An Unofficial

Harry Potter

Book of Spells.

Thomas Driks

©Copyright 2019 by Idyll Publishing
All rights reserved.
It is not legal to reproduce, duplicate, or transmit any part of this document in either electronic means or in printed format. Recording of this publication is strictly prohibited.

CONTENTS

Prologue 1
A 2
b 13
C 17
D 26
E 34
F 42
G 52
H 56
I 60
J 67
K 69
L 71
M 79

N	85
O	87
P	92
Q	100
R	102
S	110
T	117
U	120
V	122
W	126
EPILOGUE	128

PROLOGUE

Congratulations witches and wizards on your purchase! Harry Potter: Book of Spells. A comprehensive encyclopaedia of all the spells, curses, jinxes, incantations, hexes, charms, enchantments, transfigurations, summons, invocations and magical abilities used within the magical world of Harry Potter. Within these hallowed pages you'll discover every piece of magic used in the Harry Potter universe. From the dreaded Avada Kedavra curse to the little known Jelly-Legs Jinx. From Harry's go-to Expelliarmus spell to Hermione's infamous usage of the 'Wingardium Leviosa' charm. From the mind-wiping Oblivate charm to the Half-Blood Prince's violent Sectumsempra curse. You will learn about the pronunciation, the etymology, and the usage of these spells and many, many more throughout Harry Potter: Book of Spells.

Over 200 spells will be covered in this tome of magical knowledge. From basic spells any first year could perform, to the most advanced branches of dark magic only found in the dimmest corners of the Restricted Section at Hogwarts School of Witchcraft and Wizardry. Read on, young sorcerer. But be careful, don't let Filch catch you...

A

Aberto

Spell Type: Charm

Pronunciation: (Uh-bare-toe)

Description: A spell seemingly used to open objects such as doors or windows.

Accio

Spell Type: Summoning Charm

Pronunciation: (Ak-ee-oh)

Description: This charm summons an object toward the caster, potentially over a significant distance. It can be used in two ways; either by casting the charm followed by naming the object desired, or by pointing your wand at the desired object during or immediately following the incantation to "pull" the target toward the caster.

Age Line

Spell Type: Charm

Description: Creates a thin, shimmering line around the intended target that is inaccessible by those below a set age.

Aguamenti

Spell Type: Conjuration Charm

Pronunciation: (Ah-gwah-men-tee)

Description: Produces a fountain or jet of water from the wand tip.

Alarte Ascendare

Spell Type: Charm

Pronunciation: (A-lar-tey Ah-sen-deh-rey)

Description: Shoots the intended target high into the air.

Alohomora

Spell Type: Unlocking Charm

Pronunciation: (Al-loh-ha-mohr-ah)

Description: Used to open and unlock doors; it can unseal doors upon which the Locking Spell has been cast, although it is possible to bewitch doors to resist the spell.

Anapneo

Spell Type: Healing Spell

Pronunciation: (Ah-nap-nee-oh)

Description: Clears the target's airway, should they find it blocked.

Anteoculatia

Spell Type: Hex

Pronunciation: (An-tea-oh-cuh-lay-chee-a)

Description: Anteoculatia is a hex which turns a person's hair into antlers.

Anti Jinx

Spell Type: Counter Spell

Description: Prevents the effects of a jinx over one target object or animal.

Anti Cheating Spell

Spell Type: Charm

Description: Cast on parchment and quills to prevent the writer from cheating while writing answers.

Anti Disapparition

Spell Type: Jinx

Description: Used to prevent Disapparating in an area for a period of time; presumably used to trap an enemy in an area, and is related to the Anti-Apparition Charm.

Aparecium

Spell Type: Revealing Charm

Pronunciation: (Ah-par-ee-see-um)

Description: Used to prevent Disapparating in an area for a time; presumably used to trap an enemy in an area, is probably related to the Anti-Apparition Charm.

Appare Vestigium

Spell Type: Charm

Pronunciation: (App-pah-ray Vest-ee-gee-um)

Description: This spell is used to reveal footprints and track marks.

Apparate

Spell Type: Transporting Charm

Pronunciation: (Aa-puh-ray-t)

Description: Teleportation spell, used to teleport the user and anyone touching them to a location. The destination is one that the primary user has been to or seen in some fashion previously. Any items on the individuals being apparated are also teleported.

Aqua Eructo

Spell Type: Charm

Pronunciation: (A-kwa Ee-ruck-to)

Description: This spell is used to create, and control, a jet of clear water from the tip of the wand.

Arania Exumai

Spell Type: Spell

Pronunciation: (Ah-rahn-ee-a Eks-su-may)

Description: This spell is used to blast away the terrifying Acromantulas and, presumably, all other arachnids with a bright beaming of light.

Arresto Momentum

Spell Type: Charm

Pronunciation: (Ah-rest-oh Mo-men-tum)

Description: Used to decrease the velocity of a moving target; it should be noted that it can be used on multiple targets, as well as on the caster himself.

Ascendio

Spell Type: Charm

Pronunciation: (Ah-sen-dee-oh)

Description: Propels the caster high into the air.

Avada Kedavra

Spell Type: Curse

Pronunciation: (Ah-vah-dah Keh-dav-rah)

Description: One of the three "Unforgivable Curses". Causes instant death to the victim upon connecting to the intended target. This curse is accompanied by a flash of green light and a rushing noise. The use of this curse on another human results in capital punishment or life sentence in Azkaban.

*Note that this lethal curse has no known counter.

Avifors

Spell Type: Transfiguration

Pronunciation: (Ah-vi-fors)

Description: Transforms the target into a bird.

Avis

Spell Type: Conjuration Charm

Pronunciation: (Ah-vi-fors)

Description: Transforms the target into a bird.

B

Babbling

Spell Type: Curse

Description: Causes target to babble incoherently whenever they try to speak. Any attempt to cast magic with a vocal incantation while under the effect of this curse will result in a magical backlash

Baubillious

Spell Type: Charm

Pronunciation: (Baw-bill-ee-us)

Description: Produces a bolt of white light from the tip of the wand damaging the target.

Bombarda

Spell Type: Charm

Pronunciation: (Bom-bar-dah)

Description: Provokes a small explosion.

Bombarda Maxima

Spell Type: Charm

Pronunciation: (Bom-bar-dah Max-ih-mah)

Description: Create a large explosion, powerful enough to destroying entire walls.

Brackium Emendo

Spell Type: Healing Spell

Pronunciation: (Bra-keyr-um Ee-men-doh)

Description: A healing spell used to mend broken bones.

Bubble Head

Spell Type: Charm

Description: Produces a large bubble of air around the head of the user. This bubble allows the user to breathe underwater.

C

Calvario

Spell Type: Curse

Pronunciation: (Cal-vore-ee-oh)

Description: A spell that causes the victim's hair to fall out.

Cantis

Spell Type: Jinx

Pronunciation: (Can-tiss)

Description: Causes the victim to burst uncontrollably into song.

Carpe Retractum

Spell Type: Charm

Pronunciation: (Car-pay Ruh-track-tum)

Description: Produces a supernatural rope from the caster's wand, which will pull a target toward the caster.

Cascading

Spell Type: Jinx

Description: An offensive spell used to defeat multiple enemies.

Cave Inimicum

Spell Type: Charm

Pronunciation: (Kah-way Ih-nih-mih-kum)

Description: Approaching enemies are made aware of to the caster.

Cheer Up

Spell Type: Charm

Description: Causes the the person upon whom the spell is cast to become content and happy.

Cistem Aperio

Spell Type: Charm

Pronunciation: (Sis-tem Uh-pe-ree-oh)

Description: This spell was used by Tom Riddle to open the chest in which Aragog was hidden.

Colloportus

Spell Type: Charm

Pronunciation: (Cul-loh-por-tus)

Description: Locks doors, and presumably all things that can be locked.

Colloshoo

Spell Type: Hex

Pronunciation: (Cul-loh-shoe)

Description: Adheres the victim's shoes to the ground with some sort of adhesive ectoplasm.

Colovaria

Spell Type: Charm

Pronunciation: (Co-loh-va-riah)

Description: Changes the targets colour.

Confringo

Spell Type: Curse

Pronunciation: (Con-fring-goh)

Description: Causes anything that the spell comes into contact with to explode, and presumably thereafter burst into flame.

Confundo

Spell Type: Charm

Pronunciation: (Con-fun-doh)

Description: Causes the victim to become befuddled and confused.

Conjunctivitis

Spell Type: Curse

Description: It is presumed this curse causes great pain to the victim's eyes, possibly effecting their vision.

Cracker

Spell Type: Jinx

Description: This spell is used to conjure exploding wizard crackers; it can be used in duelling to harm the opponent, but the force of the explosion may also affect the caster.

Crinus Muto

Spell Type: Transfiguration

Description: This spell can change the colour and style of one's hair.

Crucio

Spell Type: Curse

Pronunciation: (Kroo-shea-oh)

Description: One of the three "Unforgivable Curses". Inflicts intense pain on the recipient of the curse; the pain is described as having hot knives being driven into the victim. The use of this curse on another human results in capital punishment or life sentence in Azkaban.

D

Defodio

Spell Type: Charm

Pronunciation: (Deh-foh-dee-oh)

Description: This spell allows the caster to gouge large chunks out of the target.

Deletrius

Spell Type: Charm

Pronunciation: (Deh-lee-tree-us)

Description: Disintegrates the target.

Densaugeo

Spell Type: Hex

Pronunciation: (Den-saw-jee-oh)

Description: This hex causes the victim's teeth to grow rapidly, but can also be used to restore lost teeth.

Descendo

Spell Type: Charm

Pronunciation: (Deh-sen-doh)

Description: Causes the target to fall downwards.

Deprimo

Spell Type: Charm

Pronunciation: (Dee-prih-moh)

Description: This spell places immense downward pressure on the target, which may result in the violent fracturing.

Diffindo

Spell Type: Charm

Pronunciation: (Dih-fin-doh)

Description: Rips, tears, shreds, or otherwise physically damages the target.

Diminuendo

Spell Type: Charm

Pronunciation: (Dim-in-yew-en-dough)

Description: Forces the target to shrink.

Dissendium

Spell Type: Charm

Pronunciation: (Dih-sen-dee-um)

Description: Used to open secret passageways.

Disillusionment

Spell Type: Charm

Description: Causes the target to blend seamlessly in with its surroundings, like a chameleon.

Draconifors

Spell Type: Transfiguration

Pronunciation: (Drah-koh-nih-fors)

Description: Transforms the target into a dragon.

Drought

Spell Type: Charm

Description: Causes puddles and ponds to dry up. Though not powerful enough to drain a body of water like a lake.

Duckifors

Spell Type: Transfiguration

Pronunciation: (Duck-lih-fors)

Description: Transforms the target into a duck.

Duro

Spell Type: Charm

Pronunciation: (Doo-roh)

Description: Transforms the target into solid stone.

E

Ears to Kumquats

Spell Type: Transfiguration

Description: This spell transforms the victim's ears into kumquats.

Ear Shrivelling Curse

Spell Type: Curse

Description: Causes the targets ears to shrivel up.

Enbublio

Spell Type: Jinx

Description: Causes the victim to inflate and explode into hundreds of bubbles; it can only be cast if an ally is using Aqua Eructo on the victim simultaneously.

Engorgio

Spell Type: Charm

Pronunciation: (En-gore-jee-oh)

Description: Causes the target to swell up in physical size.

Engorgio Skullus

Spell Type: Hex

Pronunciation: (En-gore-jee-oh Skuh-las)

Description: This hex causes the victim's skull to swell disproportionately; this spell may be a variation of the Engorgement Charm, as they share the first word of the incantation. Its counter curse is Redactum Skullus.

Entomorphis

Spell Type: Transfiguration

Pronunciation: (En-toe-morph-iss)

Description: This hex is used to transform the target into an insectoid for a short time.

Episky

Spell Type: Healing Spell

Pronunciation: (Ee-piss-key)

Description: Used to heal relatively minor injuries, such as broken bones and cartilage.

Epoximise

Spell Type: Transfiguration

Pronunciation: (Ee-pox-i-mise)

Description: Adheres one object to another, similarly to if they had been glued together.

Eructo

Spell Type: Charm

Pronunciation: (Eh-reck-toe)

Description: Used to erect a tent or other structure.

Evanesco

Spell Type: Transfiguration

Pronunciation: (Ev-an-es-koh)

Description: Vanishes the target temporarily.

Everte Statum

Spell Type: Spell

Pronunciation: (Ee-ver-tay Stah-tum)

Description: Pushes the victim backward with great force.

Expecto Patronum

Spell Type: Charm

Pronunciation: (Ecks-peck-toe Pah-troh-numb)

Description: This charm is a defensive spell which will conjure a spirit-like incarnation of their positive emotions to defend against darkcreatures; it can also send messages to other witches or wizards

Expelliarmus

Spell Type: Charm

Pronunciation: (Ex-pell-ee-arm-us)

Description: Causes whatever the victim is holding to fly away, knocks out an opponent if used too forcefully.

Expulso

Spell Type: Curse

Pronunciation: (Ex-puhl-soh)

Description: Provokes an explosion, unique in that it uses pressure to do so as apposed to heat.

F

Ferula

Spell Type: Healing Spell

Pronunciation: (Feh-roo-lah)

Description: Creates a bandage and a splint.

Fianto Duri

Spell Type: Charm

Pronunciation: (Fee-an-toe Doo-ree)

Description: Strengthens shield spells.

Fidelius

Spell Type: Charm

Description: A complex charm used to hide secret information within the soul of the charm's recipient

Fiendfyre

Spell Type: Curse

Description: Creates great spirits of fire which burn anything in its path, including nearly indestructible substances such as horcruxes. This fire is nearly impossible to control.

Finestra

Spell Type: Charm

Pronunciation: (Fi-ness-trah)

Description: Creates an aperture in a wall or window.

Finite

Spell Type: Counter Spell

Pronunciation: (Fi-nee-tay)

Description: Eliminates spell effects within the vicinity of the caster.

Finger Removal

Spell Type: Jinx

Description: Removes the targets fingers.

Firestorm

Spell Type: Charm

Description: Produces a ring of fire from the wand tip that can strike targets.

Flagrante

Spell Type: Curse

Description: Causes the curse object to burn human skin when touched.

Flagrate

Spell Type: Charm

Pronunciation: (Flug-grah-tay)

Description: Produces fiery marks from the wand tip that can be used to write.

Flipendo

Spell Type: Jinx

Pronunciation: (Flih-pen-doh)

Description: Pushes the target back, knocks out weaker enemies.

Flipendo Duo

Spell Type: Jinx

Pronunciation: (Flih-pen-doh Doo-oh)

Description: A more powerful variation of Flipendo.

Flipendo Tria

Spell Type: Jinx

Pronunciation: (Flih-pen-doh Tree-ah)

Description: An even more powerful version of Flipendo Duo; it is believed to resemble a small tornado.

Flying Charm

Spell Type: Charm

Description: This spell is cast on broomsticks and flying carpets allowing the ability to fly.

Fumos

Spell Type: Charm

Description: Used to produce a tactical cloud of dark grey smoke.

Fumos Duo

Spell Type: Charm

Description: A more powerful version of Fumos.

Furnunculus

Spell Type: Jinx

Pronunciation: (Fer-nun-kyoo-luss)

Description: Covers the target in pimples.

Fur Spell

Spell Type: Charm

Description: Causes fur to grow on the victim.

G

Geminio

Spell Type: Curse

Pronunciation: (Jeh-mih-nee-oh)

Description: Creates an identical, useless dupliacate of the target.

Glacius

Spell Type: Charm

Pronunciation: (Glay-shuss)

Description: Freezes the target within solid ice.

Glacius Duo

Spell Type: Charm

Pronunciation: (Glay-shuss Doo-oh)

Description: A stronger version of Glacius.

Glacius Tria

Spell Type: Charm

Pronunciation: (Glay-shuss Tree-ah)

Description: An even more powerful version of Glacius Duo.

Glisseo

Spell Type: Charm

Pronunciation: (Gliss-ee-oh)

Description: Causes the steps on a staircase to flatten into a slide.

H

Harmonia Nectere Passus

Spell Type: Transfiguration

Pronunciation: (Har-moh-nee-a Neck-the-ray Pass-us)

Description: Repairs a vanishing cabinet.

Herbifors

Spell Type: Transfiguration

Pronunciation: (Her-bi-fors)

Description: This spell causes flowers to sprout from the victim.

Herbivicus

Spell Type: Charm

Pronunciation: (Her-biv-i-cuss)

Description: Instantaneously grows plants to full size and maturity.

Homenum Revelio

Spell Type: Charm

Pronunciation: (Hom-eh-num Reh-veh-lee-oh)

Description: Reveals the presence of humans within the caster's vicinity.

Herbifors

Spell Type: Transfiguration

Pronunciation: (Her-bi-fors)

Description: This spell causes flowers to sprout from the victim.

Homorphus

Spell Type: Charm

Pronunciation: (Hom-or-fuss)

Description: Causes an Animagus or transfigured object to assume it natural state.

I

Illegibilus

Spell Type: Charm

Pronunciation: (I-lej-i-bill-us)

Description: Used to render text illegible.

Immobulus

Spell Type: Charm

Pronunciation: (Eem-o-bue-les)

Description: Renders living targets immobile.

Impedimenta

Spell Type: Jinx

Pronunciation: (Im-ped-ih-men-tah)

Description: This jinx is capable of tripping, freezing, binding, knocking back and generally impeding the target's progress towards the caster.

Imperio

Spell Type: Curse

Pronunciation: (Im-peer-ee-oh)

Description: One of the three "Unforgivable Curses". Places the subject in a dream-like state, in which he or she is utterly subject to the will of the caster. However, those who are strong willed may learn to resist it. The use of this curse on another human results in capital punishment or life sentence in Azkaban.

Imperturbable

Spell Type: Charm

Pronunciation: (Im-pur-choo-er-bab-el)

Description: Makes objects such as doors impenetrable.

Impervius

Spell Type: Charm

Pronunciation: (Im-pur-vee-us)

Description: Repels substances and other forces such as water to the casted target.

Inanimatus Conjurus

Spell Type: Transfiguration

Pronunciation: (In-anih-mah-tus Con-jur-us)

Description: Most likely used to conjure an inanimate object.

Incarcerous

Spell Type: Conjuration

Pronunciation: (In-car-ser-us)

Description: Binds something or someone up with ropes.

Incendio

Spell Type: Conjuration Charm

Pronunciation: (In-sen-dee-oh)

Description: Summons fire.

Incendio Duo

Spell Type: Conjuration Charm

Pronunciation: (In-sen-dee-oh)

Description: A stronger form of Incendio.

Incendio Tria

Spell Type: Conjuration Charm

Pronunciation: (In-sen-dee-oh)

Description: A more powerful version of both Incendio and Incendio Duo.

Inflatus

Spell Type: Charm

Pronunciation: (In-flay-tus)

Description: Inflates the target (inanimate or animate).

J

Jelly Fingers

Spell Type: Curse

Description: Causes the target's fingers to become almost jelly like rendering it hard for the victim to grasp and use their hands.

K

Knee Reversal

Spell Type: Hex

Description: Causes the victim's knees to appear on the opposite side of their legs.

L

Lacarnum Inflamarae

Spell Type: Charm

Pronunciation: (La-car-num In-fla-ma-ray)

Description: Propels a fiery ball of fire from the wand tip.

Langlock

Spell Type: Jinx

Pronunciation: (Lang-lock)

Description: Glues the subject's tongue to the roof of their mouth.

Lapifors

Spell Type: Transfiguration

Pronunciation: (lap-ih-forz)

Description: Transforms the target into a rabbit.

Legilimens

Spell Type: Charm

Pronunciation: (le-jil-ih-mens)

Description: Enables the caster to dive into the mind of the victim, allowing the caster to realize the memories, thoughts, and emotions of the victim.

Levicorpus

Spell Type: Jinx

Pronunciation: (Lev-ee-cor-puss)

Description: The victim is dangled upside down by their ankles.

Liberacorpus

Spell Type: Counter Spell

Pronunciation: (Lib-er-ah-cor-puss)

Description: Counter spell to Levicorpus.

Locomotor ...

Spell Type: Charm

Pronunciation: (Loh-koh-moh-tor)

Description: The spell is always used in conjunction with the name of a target, (e.g. "Locomotor Chair!"). The spell causes the selected object to rise in the air and move around at the will of the caster.

Locomotor Mortis

Spell Type: Curse

Pronunciation: (Loh-koh-moh-tor Mor-tis)

Description: Locks the victim's legs together, causing movement to be encumbered.

Locomotor Wibbly

Spell Type: Jinx

Pronunciation: (Loh-koh-moh-tor Wib-lee)

Description: Causes the victim's legs to collapse.

Lumos

Spell Type: Charm

Pronunciation: (Loo-mos)

Description: Creates a narrow beam of light that shines from the wand's tip, like a torch. To disengage the light perform the spell "Nox".

Lumos Duo

Spell Type: Charm

Pronunciation: (Loo-mos Doo-oh)

Description: Creates an intense beam of light that projects from the wand's tip and can lock-on to various targets, turn hinky punks solid and cause ghouls to retreat.

Lumos Maxima

Spell Type: Charm

Pronunciation: (Loo-mos Ma-cks-ima)

Description: Shoots a bright ball of light at the target.

Lumos Maxima

Spell Type: Charm

Pronunciation: (Loo-mos So-lem)

Description: Creates a powerful ray of light.

M

Melafors

Spell Type: Conjuration

Description: Encases the target's head in a pumpkin.

Meteolojinx Recanto

Spell Type: Counter Charm

Pronunciation: (Mee-tee-oh-loh-jinks Reh-can)

Description: Presumably causes weather effects caused by jinxes to cease.

Meteolojinx Recanto

Spell Type: Counter Charm

Pronunciation: (Mee-tee-oh-loh-jinks Reh-can)

Description: Presumably causes weather effects caused by jinxes to cease.

Mimblewimble

Spell Type: Curse

Pronunciation: (Mim-bull-wim-bull)

Description: A curse which prevents certain information from being revealed by the individual upon whom the spell is placed. The curse manifests itself by causing the tongue to temporarily curl backwards upon itself.

Mobiliarbus

Spell Type: Charm

Pronunciation: (Mo-bil-ee-ar-bus)

Description: Levitates and moves the intended object.

Mobilicorpus

Spell Type: Charm

Pronunciation: (Mo-bil-ee-cor-pus)

Description: Levitates and moves the intended object.

Morsmordre

Spell Type: Curse

Pronunciation: (Morz-mor-duh)

Description: Conjures the dark mark, a sign of the Death Eaters.

Muffliato

Spell Type: Charm

Pronunciation: (Muff-lee-ah-toe)

Description: Fills surrounding people's ears with an unidentifiable humming to hinder their hearing from nearby conversations.

Mulitcorfors

Spell Type: Transfiguration

Pronunciation: (Mull-tee-cor-fors)

Description: Used to change the colour of one's clothing.

N

Nox

Spell Type: Counter Spell

Pronunciation: (Nocks)

Description: Disengages the light produced by Lumos.

Nebulas

Spell Type: Charm

Pronunciation: (Neh-bu-lus)

Description: Conjures fog from the tip of the wand.

187

Oculus Reparo

Spell Type: Charm

Pronunciation: (Ock-u-luss Rep-are-oh)

Description: Mends eyeglasses.

Obliteration

Spell Type: Charm

Description: Removes footprints left behind.

Obliviate

Spell Type: Memory Charm

Pronunciation: (Oh-bli-vee-ate)

Description: Used to hide a memory of a particular event.

Obscuro

Spell Type: Conjuration

Pronunciation: (Ob-scy-u-roh)

Description: Used to hide a memory of a particular event.

Oppugno

Spell Type: Jinx

Pronunciation: (Oh-pug-noh)

Description: Causes animals or beings of lesser intelligence to attack.

Orbis

Spell Type: Jinx

Pronunciation: (Or-biss)

Description: Sucks the target into the ground.

Orchideous

Spell Type: Conjuration

Pronunciation: (Or-kid-ee-us)

Description: Conjures a bouquet of flowers out from the caster's wand.

P

Pack

Spell Type: Charm

Pronunciation: (Pak)

Description: Packs a bag or luggage.

Partis Temporus

Spell Type: Charm

Pronunciation: (Par-tis Temp-oar-us)

Description: Forms a temporary gap within protective magical barriers.

Periculum

Spell Type: Charm

Pronunciation: (Pur-ick-you-lum)

Description: Summons red sparks or flares shooting from the user's wand.

Permanent Stick

Spell Type: Charm

Description: Forces objects permanently stay in place.

Petrificus Totalus

Spell Type: Curse

Pronunciation: (Pe-tri-fi-cus To-tah-lus)

Description: Temporarily binds the victim's body in a position much like that of a soldier at attention; subsequently the victim will usually fall to the ground.

Piertotum Locomotor

Spell Type: Charm

Pronunciation: (Peer-toh-tum Loh-koh-moh-tor)

Description: Used to animate statues and suits of armour to do the caster's bidding.

Portus

Spell Type: Charm

Pronunciation: (Por-tus)

Description: Turns an object into a port key used for teleporting.

Prior Incantato

Spell Type: Charm

Pronunciation: (Pri-or In-can-tah-toe)

Description: Causes a echo, shadow or image of the last spell cast by a want to emanate from it.

Protego

Spell Type: Protective Charm

Pronunciation: (Pro-tay-go)

Description: A shield or protective barrier that rebounds minor to moderate jinxes, curses, and hexes upon the attacker.

Protego Diabolica

Spell Type: Protective Charm

Pronunciation: (Pro-tay-go Dia-bohl-i-ka)

Description: Summons a protective ring of fire around the caster.

Protego Horribillis

Spell Type: Protective Charm

Pronunciation: (Pro-tay-go Horr-uh-bihl-ihs)

Description: A powerful protective charm against dark magic.

Protego Maxima

Spell Type: Protective Charm

Pronunciation: (Pro-tay-go Macks-ee-ma)

Description: A powerful protective charm against dark magic. A superior version of Protego, especially in combination with multiple wizards casting on the same shield. It is said to be so powerful that it could also disintegrate intruders that came too close and attempted forced entry.

Protego Totalum

Spell Type: Protective Charm

Pronunciation: (Pro-tay-go Toe-tah-lum)

Description: Casts a protective barrier over a small area; impenetrable to pass through, with exception to the "Unforgivable Curses".

Q

Quietus

Spell Type: Charm

Pronunciation: (Kwiy-uh-tus)

Description: Returns an enchanted voice return to normal. A counter to Sonorus.

R

Redactum Skullus

Spell Type: Protective Charm

Pronunciation: (Red-ak-tum Skull-us)

Description: Shrinks the target's head. The counter spell to Engorgio Skullus.

Reducio

Spell Type: Charm

Pronunciation: (Red-oo-see-oh)

Description: Reduces the size of an object. The counter spell to Engorgio.

Reducto

Spell Type: Charm

Pronunciation: (Red-uck-toe)

Description: Destroys objects, in stronger uses disintegrates them.

Reparifors

Spell Type: Healing Charm

Description: Reverts minor magically-induced ailments, such as paralysis or poisoning.

Relashio

Spell Type: Jinx

Pronunciation: (Re-lash-ee-oh)

Description: Forces the subject to release whatever it is grasping or holding.

Rennervate

Spell Type: Charm

Pronunciation: (Ren-ur-vayt)

Description: Revives a stunned being.

Reparifarge

Spell Type: Transfiguration

Description: Reverses unsuccessful transformations.

Reparo

Spell Type: Charm

Pronunciation: (Reh-pah-roh)

Description: Repairs objects.

Repello Muggletum

Spell Type: Charm

Pronunciation: (Reh-pell-loh Mug-ul-tum)

Description: Repels muggles from entering and place of wizardry or witchcraft.

Repello Inimicum

Spell Type: Charm

Pronunciation: (Re-peh-lloh Ee-nee-mee-cum)

Description: Disintegrates the person's attempting to enter this charm.

Revelio

Spell Type: Charm

Pronunciation: (Reh-vel-ee-oh)

Description: Reveals hidden or lost objects.

Rictusempra

Spell Type: Charm

Pronunciation: (Ric-tuhs-sem-pra)

Description: Causes a severe tickling sensation, forcing targets to fall to the floor in uncontrollable laughter.

Riddikulus

Spell Type: Charm

Pronunciation: (Rih-dih-kul-lus)

Description: Forces a Boggart to take the appearance of an object the caster is concentrating on. Best results are achieved by envisioning something hilarious with intention of weakening the Boggart through comedy.

Rictusempra

Spell Type: Charm

Pronunciation: (Ric-tuhs-sem-pra)

Description: Causes a severe tickling sensation, forcing targets to fall to the floor in uncontrollable laughter.

ʆ

Scorch

Spell Type: Conjuration

Description: Produces scorching flames towards the target.

Scourgify

Spell Type: Charm

Pronunciation: (Skur-jih-fiy)

Description: A cleaning spell.

Sectumsempra

Spell Type: Curse

Pronunciation: (Sec-tum Semp-rah)

Description: Creates large, blood-oozing gashes on the subject as if they had been slashed by a sword.

Serpentsortia

Spell Type: Charm

Pronunciation: (Ser-pen-sor-shah)

Description: Summons a slithering serpent from the spell-casters wand.

Silencio

Spell Type: Charm

Pronunciation: (Sih-len-see-oh)

Description: Forces silence upon the target.

Slugulus Eructo

Spell Type: Curse

Description: A blast of green light strikes the subject, who will then vomit slugs for ten minutes. The size of the vomited slugs decrease with time.

Sonorous

Spell Type: Charm

Pronunciation: (Soh-nohr-uhs)

Description: Sonorous emits a magnified roar from the tip of wand. Similar to the likes of a megaphone.

Specialis Revelio

Spell Type: Charm

Pronunciation: (Speh-see-ah-lis Reh-vel-ee-oh)

Description: Uncovers an objects hidden secrets or magical properties.

Spongify

Spell Type: Charm

Pronunciation: (Spun-jih-fy)

Description: Softens the target.

Steleus

Spell Type: Hex

Pronunciation: (Stay-lee-us)

Description: Causes the victim to sneeze for a short period of time.

Stupefy

Spell Type: Charm

Pronunciation: (Stoo-puh-fye)

Description: Stuns victims. If used too forcefully, it will knock the victim into an unconscious state.

T

Tarantallegra

Spell Type: Curse

Pronunciation: (Tuh-rahn-tuh-lehg-rah)

Description: Forces the victim's legs to dance uncontrollably.

Tentaclifors

Spell Type: Transfiguration

Pronunciation: (Ten-tah-cul-ee-fors)

Description: Transfigures the victim's head into a tentacle.

Tergeo

Spell Type: Charm

Pronunciation: (Tur-jee-oh)

Description: Siphons liquid.

Titillando

Spell Type: Hex

Description: Tickles and weakens target.

Trip

Spell Type: Jinx

Description: Used to trip or impede the targets movement.

Ս

Unbreakable

Spell Type: Charm

Description: Renders something unbreakable.

Unbreakable Vow

Spell Type: Charm

Description: Any vow taken by a witch or wizard under this spell is to be inviolable. If the charm is broken, the consequence is death.

V

Ventus

Spell Type: Jinx

Pronunciation: (Ven-tus)

Description: A forceful blast of wind is cast from the end of the wand, knocking back objects.

Ventus Duo

Spell Type: Jinx

Pronunciation: (Ven-tus Doo-oh)

Description: A superior version of the Ventus Jinx.

Vera Verto

Spell Type: Transfiguration

Pronunciation: (Vair-uh-vair-toh)

Description: Turns animals into water in the form of goblets.

Verdimillious

Spell Type: Charm

Pronunciation: (Ver-dim-mill-lee-us)

Description: Shoots green sparks out from the wand tip.

Verdimillious Duo

Spell Type: Charm

Pronunciation: (Ver-dim-mill-lee-us Doo-oh)

Description: A stronger set of sparks are cast compared to Verdimillious.

Vulnera Sanentur

Spell Type: Healing Charm

Pronunciation: (Vul-nur-ah Sahn-en-tur)

Description: Causes wounds and gashes to heal, any lost blood is also rejuvenated.

1126

Waddiwasi

Spell Type: Charm

Pronunciation: (Wah-dee-wah-see)

Description: Launches small objects through the air.

Wingardium Leviosa

Spell Type: Charm

Pronunciation: (Win-gar-dee-um Lev-ee-oh-sa)

Description: Levitates and manipulates the target objects movement.

EPILOGUE

You've done it! You've completed the Harry Potter: Book of Spells. You've learnt every single spell, curse, enchantment and charm ever used in the magical world of Harry Potter. You're wiser than Dumbledore. More powerful than Lord Voldemort. More cunning than Professor Snape and more knowledgeable than Hermione Granger. You are the greatest muggle-born who has ever lived. But what will you do with this new found awareness and power? Will you assist Harry and the rest of the Order of the Phoenix in taking down Voldemort and his hordes of Death Eaters? Will you aid the Dark Lord, joining his dark ranks in his attempted conquest of Hogwarts School of Witchcraft and Wizardry? Or will you choose neither, and live a life of obscurity like the strange and eccentric Xenophilius Lovegood? The choice is yours. You have all the power. Go forth with this new knowledge, and begin your next chapter in the wizarding world with everything you have learnt in Harry Potter: Book of Spells.

Printed in Great Britain
by Amazon